WHAT ON EARTH IS A
TUATARA

JENNY TESAR

 A BLACKBIRCH PRESS BOOK
WOODBRIDGE, CONNECTICUT

Published by Blackbirch Press, Inc.
One Bradley Road, Suite 104
Woodbridge, CT 06525

©1994 Blackbirch Press, Inc.
First Edition

Printed in Hong Kong

10 9 8 7 6 5 4 3 2 1

PUBLISHER'S THANKS
Blackbirch Press would like to give special thanks to Ron Goellner, Curator of Reptiles at the St. Louis Zoo, for his valuable help on this project. In addition to supplying a number of photographs, Mr. Goellner also reviewed the manuscript and offered advice that greatly improved this book.

Photo Credits
Cover, title page: ©Tom McHugh/Photo Researchers, Inc.
Pages 4—5: ©Doug Wechsler/Animals Animals; page 7: ©Ron Goellner; page 9: ©Asa C. Thorensen/Photo Researchers, Inc.; page 10: ©Brian Enting/Photo Researchers, Inc.; page 12: ©Ron Goellner; page 13: ©Ron Goellner; page 15: ©Ron Goellner; page 16: ©Ron Goellner; page 17: ©Joe McDonald/Animals Animals; page 19: ©Ron Goellner; pages 20—21: ©Ron Goellner; page 23: ©Ron Goellner; page 25: ©Zig Leszczynski/Animals Animals; page 26: ©Ron Goellner; page 27: ©Ron Goellner; pages 28-29: ©Ron Goellner. Map by Blackbirch Graphics, Inc.

Library of Congress Cataloging-in-Publication Data
Tesar, Jenny E.
What on earth is a tuatara? / Jenny Tesar. — 1st ed.
  p.   cm. — (What on earth series)
  Includes bibliographical references (p.   ) and index.
  ISBN 1-56711-092-4 : $12.95
  1. Tuatara—Juvenile literature. [1. Tuatara. 2. Reptiles.]
I. Title. II. Series.
QL666.R48T47   1994
597.9'45—dc20
                                                    94-27857
                                                        CIP
                                                         AC

What does it look like?

Where does it live?

What does it eat?

How does it reproduce?

How does it survive?

TURN THESE PAGES AND FIND OUT!

TUATARAS ARE RARE REPTILES THAT
ARE ONLY FOUND ON ISLANDS OFF THE
COAST OF NEW ZEALAND.

A tuatara is a very unusual, and very rare reptile. Some people say tuataras look like a cross between a lizard and a dinosaur. Tuataras are only found on small islands off the coast of New Zealand.

The tuatara was named by the Maoris, who were the first people to settle in New Zealand. The name tuatara means "peaks on the back" in the Maori language. This refers to the spiny crest along a tuatara's back.

The tuatara looks like a large lizard. But it is a distant relative of lizards. Its skull, teeth, and other body parts are very different from those of lizards.

The tuatara is a "living fossil." It is the only surviving member of an ancient group of reptiles called beak-heads. These reptiles had a large beak, or snout. All the other beak-heads lived millions of years ago. They lived before and during the time when dinosaurs roamed the Earth. We know of beak-heads from fossils. Fossils are parts of dead plants or animals that have been preserved in rocks and other materials for millions of years.

THE TUATARA IS THE ONLY LIVING MEMBER OF AN ANCIENT GROUP OF
REPTILES CALLED BEAK-HEADS.

There are more than 6,000 kinds, or species, of living reptiles. They include turtles, crocodiles, alligators, lizards, snakes—and two species of tuataras.

Each species in the animal world has its own scientific name. The scientific name for the two species of tuataras are *Sphenodon punctatus and Sphenodon guntheri.* The word *sphenodon* comes from ancient Greek and Latin words meaning "pointed wedge tooth." A tuatara's teeth are shaped like wedges. That is, the tip of each tooth is much narrower than the part attached to the jaw.

THERE ARE MORE THAN 6,000 SPECIES OF REPTILES, BUT ONLY TWO KNOWN SPECIES OF TUATARA.

A male tuatara may grow to be 25 inches (65 centimeters) long from its nose to the tip of its tail. It may weigh more than 2 pounds (900 grams). Females are, on the average, smaller than males and weigh less.

The tuatara's body is covered with scales, which keep its body from drying out. The crest

along a tuatara's back is made of specialized
scales. When a tuatara is excited or frightened,
it raises and stiffens its crest to warn or scare
an enemy.

A tuatara has two normal eyes. It also has a
third "eye" under the skin on the top of its head.
The scale that covers this eye can be seen in very
young tuataras. Scientists do not know the
purpose of this eye, but they do not think it can
really function.

LIKE MOST REPTILES, A TUATARA'S BODY IS COVERED IN SCALES.
SPECIAL SCALES ON THE BACK FORM A TUATARA'S RECOGNIZABLE
CREST.

Australia

New
Zealand

TUATARA TERRITORY

TUATARAS LIVE IN UNDERGROUND HOMES CALLED
BURROWS, WHICH ALSO SHADE THEM FROM THE
SUN ON HOT DAYS.

Tuataras live on small rocky islands that are covered with trees and shrubs. They live both on and in the ground. They use their claws to dig underground homes called burrows. Sometimes, they make their homes in burrows dug by petrels and other seabirds.

Tuataras are active mainly at night. They spend most of the hot daytime resting in their burrows. Sometimes, they come out on warm days to sunbathe.

THE COASTLINE OF STEPHENS ISLAND NEAR THE NEW ZEALAND MAINLAND IS HOME TO MANY TUATARAS. IT IS MOSTLY DRY AND ROCKY.

Tuataras are most plentiful on islands that have large populations of seabirds. The seabirds cover the ground with droppings, or wastes. Many kinds of insects, such as beetles, feed on the droppings. The insects, in turn, become food for tuataras. Tuataras also eat spiders, sow bugs, earthworms, and snails. They eat bird eggs and baby birds, too.

A tuatara hunts on the ground. It depends on its large brown eyes to find food. When a tuatara sees an insect or other prey crawling nearby, it quickly grabs the prey with its jaws.

TUATARAS FEED MAINLY ON INSECTS, SPIDERS, AND OTHER SMALL CREATURES THAT CRAWL ALONG THE GROUND.

Tuataras share their island homes with many other animals. Large numbers of seabirds build nests and raise their young on the islands. Small lizards called geckos and skinks scramble over the rocks. Tiny frogs found nowhere else on Earth live under rock piles.

Almost as unusual as the tuatara is the kiwi. This roly-poly bird has brown, hair-like feathers and a very long beak. Its wings are very tiny and it cannot fly. The kiwi waddles about at night on its short legs, hunting for insects and worms. Like the tuatara, it lives in a burrow.

GECKOS, SUCH AS THE
ONE ON THE LEFT, AND
SKINKS (BELOW) ARE
OTHER REPTILES THAT
SHARE THE TUATARA'S
ISLAND HABITAT.

A FEMALE TUATARA
WATCHES FOR POSSIBLE
INTRUDERS. KIORE AND
NORWAY RATS ARE AMONG
THE ONLY ANIMALS THAT
POSE A REAL THREAT TO
TUATARAS.

Long ago, tuataras lived throughout New Zealand. They did not have many enemies. But when people arrived, they brought along rats, dogs, and other mammals. These mammals hunted tuataras and destroyed their environment. Today, tuataras survive only on about 30 small islands off the coast of New Zealand.

On some of these small islands, there are no important enemies of tuataras. On other islands, there are Norway rats and kiore. Kiore are rats that Maoris originally brought to New Zealand from Polynesia. Kiore eat mainly plant matter. But it seems that Norway rats and kiore may also eat tuatara eggs and maybe even young tuataras. On islands with these rats, the number of tuataras is decreasing.

If something frightens a female tuatara, she quickly runs into her burrow. Male tuataras are just as quick to take action. A male tuatara will face an enemy and try to scare it. To do this, he will raise his crest and bark.

If an enemy grabs a tuatara by its tail, the tail may break off at a special place. Then the enemy has the tail...but the tuatara runs away! Later, the tuatara's tail will slowly grow back.

A MALE TUATARA USES ITS CREST TO TRY TO FRIGHTEN AWAY POSSIBLE ENEMIES.

To survive, a species must reproduce. That is, it must make more creatures of the same kind. Otherwise, the species will become extinct, or cease to exist.

Among tuataras, the first step in reproduction is mating. This takes place during the New Zealand summer. During mating, a male tuatara presses against a female. A fluid containing reproductive cells called sperm flows from an opening in the male's body. The fluid flows into an opening in the female's body.

Some of the sperm will join with eggs in the female's body. When a sperm and an egg unite, the egg is said to be fertilized. A fertilized egg will develop into a baby tuatara.

AS PART OF THEIR MATING RITUAL, MALE TUATARAS "DISPLAY" TO FEMALES BY RAISNG THEIR CRESTS.

BEFORE SHE LAYS HER EGGS, A FEMALE TUATARA DIGS A HOLE IN THE GROUND. ONCE THE EGGS ARE LAID, THEY ARE LEFT ON THEIR OWN.

In spring, about 10 months after mating, a female tuatara digs a hole in the ground. She lays from 5 to 15 fertilized eggs in the hole. Then she covers the hole with soil and crawls away. Neither she nor the male give any more care to the eggs.

Each fertilized egg has a thick shell that protects it. It has a large yolk, which contains food for the developing tuatara.

Baby tuataras are born about 15 months after the eggs are laid. Each baby has a sharp egg-breaker called an "egg tooth" on the top of its nose. It uses this pointy bump to break open its eggshell.

A HATCHLING TUATARA IS QUITE SMALL, USUALLY ABOUT 2 INCHES (5 CENTIMETERS) LONG.

At birth, a tuatara is a little over 2 inches (5 centimeters) long. It grows slowly. It does not become an adult that is able to mate until it is about 20 years old.

AT 4 TO 5 YEARS OF AGE, A TUATARA IS ONLY ABOUT 8 TO 9 INCHES (20 CENTIMETERS) LONG.

A 7-YEAR-OLD TUATARA STILL FITS INTO THE PALM OF AN ADULT
HUMAN HAND.

Even though it takes them a relatively long time
to develop, most tuataras can live for many years.
Many wildlife scientists who have studied reptiles
believe that, on the average, tuataras may live for
more than 100 years.

EVEN THOUGH THEY HAVE BEEN ON EARTH FOR MILLIONS OF YEARS, TUATARAS WILL NOT SURVIVE IF THEY ARE NOT PROTECTED BY HUMANS.

Long ago, people ate tuataras and their eggs. Today, killing tuataras and taking their eggs is illegal.

Because tuataras are very rare, they are carefully protected by the New Zealand government. Scientists try to keep the islands on which tuataras live free of dogs, cats, rats, goats, and other animals that might hunt tuataras.

Tuataras have lived on Earth for millions of years. But today only a small number of tuataras still exist. It is only with the help of humans that these fascinating animals will be able to survive for many millions of years into the future.

Glossary

burrow A hole in the ground made by an animal, often used as its home.

egg A female reproductive cell.

environment Surroundings; natural habitat.

fertilization The joining of a male sex cell, called a sperm, and a female sex cell, called an egg. Fertilization is a part of reproduction.

fossils Preserved remains of organisms that lived long ago.

prey Animals that are caught and eaten by other animals, called predators.

reproduction Making more creatures of the same kind.

scientific name A name for a species that is the same everywhere in the world. It has two parts. For example, the scientific name for one species of tuatara is *Sphenodon punctatus*.

species A group of living things that are closely related to one another. Members of a species can reproduce with one another. There are two known species of tuataras.

sperm Male reproductive cells.

Further Reading

Caitlin, Stephen. *Discovering Reptiles &
  Amphibians.* Mahwah, NJ: Troll, 1990.
Fagan, Elizabeth G. *Rand McNally Children's Atlas
  of World Wildlife.* Chicago: Rand McNally, 1993.
Few, Roger. *Macmillan Animal Encyclopedia for
  Children.* New York: Macmillan Child Group, 1991.
Keyworth, Valerie. *New Zealand: Land of the Long
  White Cloud.* New York: Dillon, 1990.
Losito, Linda. *Reptiles and Amphibians.* New York:
  Facts On File, 1989.
Ricciuti, Edward R. *Reptiles.* Woodbridge, CT:
  Blackbirch Press, 1993.
Richardson, Joy. *Reptiles.* New York: Franklin Watts,
  1993.
Spinelli, Eileen. *Reptiles.* Lake Forest, IL: Forest
  House, 1992.
Steele, Philip. *Extinct Reptiles: And Those in
  Danger of Extinction.* Chicago: Watts, 1991.

Index